MEDITERRANEAN

Colophon

www.rebo-publishers.com – info@rebo-publishers.com

This 2nd edition reprinted 2004

Design, editing and production: Minkowsky Graphics, Enkhuizen, The Netherlands

Translation and adaptation: American Pie, London, UK and Sunnyvale, California, USA

ISBN 90 366 1475 9

Mediterranean

around the Mediterranean, sun, sea, and shore for

creative cooking

Foreword

Just imagine you are bobbing along in a boat along the coast of the Mediterranean. The sun is beating down. You let yourself glide lazily into the water, swim alongside the boat to the shore, tie the boat up, and decide to linger in this little port. You find a little restaurant in the harbor, choose a table, and let the owner recommend the dish of the day. And the food that lands on your plate – is unsurpassed! Or it could be. This book consists of a collection of recipes from the lands bordering the Mediterranean, where people still really know how to live. You will enjoy to the full everything from Classic bouillabaisse and Turkish tabbouleh to Baked chicken with Parmesan and Shrimp with provençal tomato salsa.

Abbreviations

tbsp = tablespoon

tsp = teaspoon

g = gram

kg = kilogram

fl oz = fluid ounce

lb = pound

oz = ounce

ml = milliliter

l = liter

°C = degree Celsius

°F = degree Fahrenheit

Where three measurements are given, the first is the American cup measure.

Serves **10–12**

Method

Rinse the heads, bones, and trimmings. Heat the olive oil in a deep saucepan and add the fish heads and bones. Cook over a high heat, stirring constantly, until the fish begins to break down, scraping up anything that sticks to the bottom of the pan, about 20 minutes. Add the wine and simmer, stirring well. Add the prepared vegetables, herbs, bay leaves and water and simmer for 30 minutes, skimming any scum off the surface as it appears. After 30 minutes, strain the cooking liquid thoroughly, pressing on the solids to extract as much liquid as possible. Return to the heat for a further 20 minutes then add salt and pepper to taste. Set aside.

To make the soup, heat the olive oil and add the sliced leeks, fennel, shallots, potatoes and saffron and cook over a medium heat until all the vegetables are golden and soft, about 20 minutes. Add the squashed canned tomatoes and reserved fish liquid and bring the soup to the boil. Add salt and pepper to taste.

Add the fish fillets, shrimp, and mussels and simmer for 10 minutes. Add the cleaned squid and parsley and stir gently. Remove the soup from the heat and cover. Allow to rest for 10 minutes.

To make the rouille, slice the bell peppers, discarding seeds and ribs, and roast them by placing them, skin side up, under a hot broiler until blistered. Place the bell pepper pieces in a plastic bag until cool then peel and discard the skin. Chop all the ingredients, except the olive oil and salt and pepper, in a food processor, taking care not to over-process. When the ingredients are well mixed add enough olive oil, salt and pepper to make a flavorsome paste.

Brush the sliced sourdough bread with olive oil and broil until golden on both sides. Rub a clove of garlic over each golden slice. To serve, place a slice of bread on the bottom of each soup bowl and ladle the hot soup over it. Make sure mussels, shrimp, and squid are distributed evenly. Add 1 tbsp/15ml rouille to the bowl and hand the rest of the rouille separately.

Ingredients

Broth:

4 lb 8 oz/2kg fish heads and bones, 4 tbsp/60ml olive oil, 3 cups/24 fl oz750ml dry white wine, 4 carrots, peeled and sliced, 2 leeks, washed and sliced, 2 onions, peeled and sliced, 3 ribs celery, sliced, 6 tomatoes, chopped, 1 tsp/5g peppercorns, 1 bunch thyme, tied together, 1 bunch parsley, tied together, 1 bunch dill, tied together, 4 fresh bayleaves, 8 cups/3½ pints/2 l water

Classic bouillabaisse

Soup:

2 tbsp olive oil, 2 large leeks, washed and sliced, 1 large fennel bulb, finely sliced, 6 shallots, peeled and sliced, 3 medium potatoes, peeled and diced, large pinch of saffron threads, 2 x 400g cans Italian-style tomatoes, salt and pepper to taste, 2 kg assorted fish fillets, diced, 500g large raw prawns, peeled, 800g mussels, scrubbed and rinsed, 400g small squid, cleaned, 1 bunch parsley, chopped, 1 loaf sourdough bread, a little olive oil , 1 clove of garlic

Rouille:

2 large red bell peppers, 1 cup breadcrumbs, 3 cloves garlic, 1 cup liquid from the soup, 2 small, red chili peppers, 1 tsp red wine vinegar, olive oil, salt and pepper to taste

Serves **4–6**

Method

1. To make the soup, heat the oil in a large heavy-based saucepan, then add the onion, potato, carrot, and yellow pepper. Cook, uncovered, for 5 minutes over a medium heat, stirring occasionally, until the vegetables just start to brown.
2. Add the broth, celery and zucchini (courgettes) and bring to the boil. Cover and simmer for 10 minutes or until the vegetables are tender. Stir in the tomatoes and tomato paste, and season generously. Simmer, uncovered, for 10 minutes.
3. Meanwhile, make the pesto: place the green onions (scallions), Parmesan, and oil in a food processor and process to a smooth paste. Ladle the soup into bowls and top with a tablespoon of the pesto.

Provençal-style soup with green onion pesto

Ingredients

2 tbsp/30ml extra virgin olive oil

1 onion, chopped

1 medium potato, peeled, and chopped

1 carrot, chopped

1 yellow bell pepper, deseeded, and chopped

2¼ cups/18fl oz/500ml garlic and herb broth

2 celery sticks, chopped

2 zucchini (courgettes), chopped

1¾oz/14oz/400g can chopped tomatoes

1 tbsp/15ml tomato purée

sea salt and freshly ground black pepper

Pesto:

6 green onions (scallions), roughly chopped, including green parts

¼ cup/2oz/50g grated Parmesan

4 tbsp/60ml extra virgin olive oil

mediterranean

Serves **6**

Method

Add the dried porcini to the boiling water and set aside. When the mushrooms have softened, remove them from the mushroom water and set them aside. Strain the mushroom liquid through a paper towel or cheesecloth-lined sieve to separate sand and grit, and reserve the liquid. Heat the olive oil and add the garlic, leek, and shallots, and cook until golden, about 3 minutes.

Add all the fresh mushrooms, thinly sliced, and cook over a very high heat until the mushrooms soften and their liquid evaporates, about 6 minutes. Reserve a few mushroom pieces for a garnish.

Sprinkle with the flour and stir well to enable the flour to be absorbed.

Add the broth and the porcini mushrooms together with the soaking liquid and bring to the boil, stirring frequently.

Once the soup is boiling, reduce the heat to a simmer and cook for 30 minutes.

Add the cream and simmer for a further 5 minutes or until slightly thickened.

Add half the chopped parsley, the sliced basil, and oregano, and season to taste with salt and pepper.

To serve, ladle into individual bowls, sprinkle with extra parsley, reserved mushrooms, some nutmeg, and a little extra cream if desired.

Ingredients

2tbsp/20g dried porcini (cep) mushrooms

½ cup/4fl oz/125ml boiling water

2 tbsp/30ml olive oil

2 cloves of garlic, minced

1 leek, cleaned and chopped

6 shallots, chopped

1½ cups/10oz/300g button mushrooms

5 cups/1¼ lb/500g mixed mushrooms (such as porcini, shiitake, oyster, and portobello)

2 tbsp/1oz/25g all-purpose (plain) flour

4 cups/16fl oz/450ml chicken, beef, or vegetable broth

1 cup/8fl oz/250ml thick cream

6 tbsp/90g chopped flat-leaved parsley

30 basil leaves, sliced

1 tbsp/15g fresh oregano

salt, pepper and nutmeg to taste

Porcini mushroom soup

Note:

To make a lower fat version of this delicious soup, use evaporated skim milk instead of the cream.

Method

Wash tomatoes. Use the stem end of the tomatoes as the base, as they will then sit better in the oven and on the plate. Slice almost all the way through the tomato at about ⅛ in/½ cm from the top , taking care to leave the "lid" attached.
Flip back the lid and scoop out the pulp with a teaspoon, leaving the walls intact.
Sprinkle each cavity with a pinch of sugar, place in a baking pan, and set aside.
Place tomato pulp into a saucepan with salt, pepper and ½ tsp/2.5g sugar. Simmer until the pulp is soft. Press through a sieve, rubbing with the back of a wooden spoon. Discard the seeds. Set purée aside.
In a saucepan, heat half of the oil (¼ cup/2 fl oz/50ml) and fry the onion until soft.
Add pine nuts and stir for 2 minutes. Add rice, stir a little to coat grains with oil, then add currants, hot water, parsley, mint and ½ cup/4fl oz/125ml of the tomato purée. Bring to the boil, reduce the heat, cover, and simmer gently 10–12 minutes, or until all liquid is absorbed.
Spoon rice mixture into tomatoes, allowing a little room for rice to swell. Replace lid.
Pour remaining tomato purée over the tomatoes and add about ½ cup/4fl oz/125ml water to the pan.
Spoon remaining oil over the tomatoes and place, uncovered, into a preheated moderate oven for 40 minutes. Check the liquid content and add a little extra water if necessary. Some tomatoes are very watery and there may be too much liquid in the pan, in which case, cook for longer to evaporate the water, until tomatoes are surrounded by a thick tomato sauce.
Serve hot or cold. If served cold, allow the tomatoes to cool in the sauce.

Tomatoes yemistes (stuffed tomatoes)

Ingredients

12 medium-sized ripe tomatoes
a little sugar, salt and pepper
½ tsp/2.5 g sugar, plus extra for sprinkling
½ cup/4fl oz/125ml olive oil
1 large onion, minced
¼ cup/2 oz/50g pine nuts
1½ cups/ short grain rice

mediterranean

½/4 oz/125g cup currants

1½ cups/12fl oz/350ml hot water

2 tbsp/30g chopped flat-leaved parsley

2 tbsp/30g chopped mint

Method

Heat the oven to 370°F/190°C. Season duck breast with a little salt and pepper. Heat peanut oil in a pan until almost smoking then add the duck breast, skin side down, and cook on a high heat until the skin is a deep caramel color. Transfer the pan to the oven and cook for 7–10 minutes. (Do not turn the duck breasts over.) Remove the pan from the oven and remove the breasts from pan, keeping them warm. Drain and discard the excess fat. Add the butter and, when it begins to bubble, add the thyme leaves then the honey. When simmering, replace duck breasts, skin side up.

Cook for a further minute on low heat then remove pan altogether.

Whisk together the lemon juice, walnut oil, salt and pepper, and the pan juices, and mix well. Toss the lettuce leaves and pomegranate with a little of the dressing. Divide the lettuce leaves between the plates and garnish with tomatoes. Slice the duck breast and arrange it around the salad, drizzling any excess honey sauce over the duck slices. Garnish with basil leaves and serve.

Ingredients

3 duck breasts, skin on

salt and pepper

1 tbsp/15ml peanut oil

2 tsp/10g butter

1 sprig thyme, leaves picked from the stalk

2 tbsp/30ml honey

1 tbsp/15ml lemon juice

2 tbsp/30ml walnut oil

fine gray sea salt and cracked black pepper

3 cups/7oz/200g mixed salad leaves

1 pomegranate (optional), seeds and pulp scooped out

6 large cherry tomatoes

basil leaves to garnish

Salad of sautéed duck with thyme and honey

mediterranean

Makes **8**

Method

To make the bruschetta base, cut the bread into thick slices and toast both sides until crisp and golden. Rub one side of each bread slice with the garlic.

Tomato, garlic, and basil topping

Combine the chopped tomato, garlic, and shredded basil. Spoon on top of the toasts and sprinkle with cracked black pepper.

Sardine and ricotta bruschetta

Mash the cream cheese with the lemon rind and thyme. Drain the sardines and leave them whole. Thickly spread the toasts with cream cheese and top with two halves of sardine. Add a piece of thinly-sliced lemon for garnish.

Tomato, garlic, and basil bruschetta **Sardine** and ricotta bruschetta

Ingredients

1 loaf ciabatta or 1 French stick

2 cloves of garlic, halved

Tomato, garlic, and basil

2 vine-ripened tomatoes, chopped

1 clove of garlic, crushed

1 tbsp basil, finely shredded

cracked black pepper

1 loaf ciabatta or 1 French stick

2 cloves of garlic, halved

Ricotta and sardine

⅓ cup/3oz/100g reduced-fat ricotta cheese

1 lemon, rind grated

1 tbsp/15g fresh thyme, chopped

2 x 4oz/125g cans sardines, drained, halved, and bones removed

½ lemon, very thinly sliced

mediterranean

Serves **8**

Method

Peel and slice the onions into rounds. Heat the butter or oil and sauté the garlic and onions until they are shiny and golden brown, about 15 minutes. Add the flour and stir to allow the flour to absorb the butter residue.

Add the sugar, beef broth, water, and wine and bring to the boil then simmer for 45 minutes. Add the sherry and simmer 5 minutes more. Add salt and pepper to taste.

Toast the bread until golden. Meanwhile, mix the two cheeses and parsley in a bowl. Place 1 heaping tbsp/20g of cheese mixture on each round of toast and broil under a hot broiler until cheese is hot and bubbling.

Place one round of bread in each soup bowl and then ladle boiling soup over it. The toast should rise to the surface. Serve immediately.

Ingredients

8 large onions

⅓ cup/3½oz/100g butter or olive oil

2 cloves of garlic, minced

1½ tbsp/20g all-purpose flour

1 tbsp/15g sugar

4 cups/1¾ pints/1 l beef broth

2–3 cups water

Traditional French onion soup

½ cup/4fl oz/125ml red wine

4 tbsp/60ml sherry or port

salt and pepper to taste

8 slices whole-wheat or rye bread

½ cup/4oz/125g grated Gruyère cheese

½ cup/4oz/125g grated Parmesan

½ cup/4oz/125g minced parsley

Method

Heat the broth in a saucepan and allow to simmer.

Heat the olive oil in a second saucepan and add the onion, garlic, and chopped red peppers and cook until softened. Add the roughly chopped tomatoes and tomato paste and cook over a medium heat for 10 minutes. Purée this mixture then return it to the saucepan.

Remove the crusts from the bread and discard them. Dice the bread into small cubes.

Add the broth to the tomato mixture, together with the bread, basil, and salt and pepper to taste.

Cover and simmer for about 45 minutes then stir vigorously with a wooden spoon to break up the bread cubes.

Serve either hot or at room temperature, with a few extra pieces of basil and some freshly ground black pepper.

Ingredients

7 cups/3 pints/1.75l vegetable, chicken, or beef broth

6 tbsp/90ml olive oil

2 onions, peeled and roughly chopped

3 cloves of garlic, minced

2 red bell peppers, finely chopped

5 cups/2 lb 12 oz/1.2kg ripe beefsteak tomatoes

2 tbsp/30ml tomato paste

14oz/400g stale whole-wheat or rye bread

¼ cup/2oz/50g fresh basil leaves, torn

salt and freshly ground pepper to taste

Pappa al pomodoro

Tip

For a smoother texture, purée the soup briefly to break up some of the bread cubes but be careful not to over-process.

Serves **4**

Method

1. Preheat the broiler to high. Toss the bread in the oil to coat evenly and spread out on a baking sheet. Broil for 1–2 minutes, or until golden, turning occasionally, then leave to cool for 10 minutes.

2. Meanwhile, make the dressing. Heat the oil in a small saucepan and fry the chili pepper, stirring, for 1 minute or until softened but not browned. Remove from the heat, leave to cool slightly, then add the pesto and vinegar. Whisk with a fork and season.

3. Mix the toasted bread with the tomatoes, onion, and feta. Scatter the basil over the salad. Spoon over the dressing and toss lightly to combine.

Tomato and bread salad with pesto dressing

Ingredients

1 French bread stick, cubed

2 tbsp/30 fl oz olive oil

3 large tomatoes, cut into 1in/2½cm chunks

1 small red onion, thinly sliced

⅓cup/3½oz/100g feta, crumbled

handful of fresh basil leaves, torn

Dressing:

3 tbsp/45ml olive oil

1 red chili pepper, deseeded and finely chopped

2 tbsp/30ml red pesto

2 tbsp/30ml red wine vinegar

salt and black pepper

mediterranean

Serves **4**

Method

1. Put the octopus in a large saucepan without adding water. Sprinkle with salt, cover, and let cook in its own juices over a low heat (for about 45 minutes).
2. Four times during the cooking, lift the octopus out with a fork and dip into a pan of boiling water. Then rinse the octopus under cold water and return it to the saucepan to continue cooking.
3. Heat the olive oil in an ovenproof casserole dish and gently fry in it the onion, garlic, tomatoes and chili powder for about 10 minutes, or until the onion is no longer transparent. Add the potatoes and cook about 5 minutes. Add the octopus and enough of its cooking liquid to cover the contents of the casserole. Add salt as desired, and let the dish cook gently, uncovered, for about 30 minutes (or until the potatoes are tender and the sauce is largely reduced).
4. Finally, add the cooked peas to the casserole and heat through. Serve the octopus and vegetables straight from the casserole.

Octopus with potatoes and peas

Ingredients

2¼lb/1kg octopus, cleaned and skinned

salt

150ml olive oil

1 large onion (chopped)

4 cloves of garlic, chopped

1¾ cups14oz/400g canned tomatoes

¼ tsp/1.25g ground chili powder

5 cups/1¼ lb/500g potatoes, peeled and thickly sliced

1 cup/8 oz/250g cooked peas

Serves **4**

Method

Place bacon in a cold frying pan. Stir over low heat for 5 minutes or until bacon is lightly golden. Add garlic and mushrooms, and cook stirring for 3 minutes or until tender.

Whisk eggs, cream, cheese, and pepper together in a large bowl.

Meanwhile, cook fettucini according to instructions on the package, then drain. While still hot, add to egg mixture, and stir quickly until combined. Add hot bacon mixture, stir until combine.

Fettucini with creamy bacon & mushroom sauce

Ingredients

6 slices bacon, cut into strips
4 cloves of garlic, crushed
1 cup/4oz/125g button mushrooms, sliced
4 eggs
⅓ cup/3½ fl oz/100ml heavy (thick) cream
⅔ cup/5oz/150g freshly grated parmesan cheese
freshly ground black pepper
14oz/400g green and white fettucini

Tip

It is important that the fettucini are very hot as it is this heat that will thicken the egg mixture to form a delicious creamy sauce.

Serves **8 as an appetizer**

Method

If necessary, cut prosciutto slices in half lengthways.

Neatly wrap small melon slices in prosciutto and skewer with toothpicks.

Stuff prunes with the cheese pieces. Neatly wrap the prunes in prosciutto.

Ingredients

16 thin prosciutto slices

16 slices small melon (ogen, honeydew, or crenshaw)

16 pieces creamy blue cheese

16 pitted prunes

toothpicks

Air-dried prosciutto roll ups

Tip

Chopped walnuts can be added to the blue cheese. Use fresh figs instead of melon. Prosciutto can also be rolled around bocconcini (miniature mozzarella) and tomato.
Prosciutto can be replaced with thin sliced of glazed ham.

Serves **4**

Method

1. Preheat the oven to 350°F/180°C. Place half the garlic head and half the lime wedges in a roasting pan. Lightly crush the cardamom, cumin, and cloves with a pestle and mortar and add to the pan. Tuck a few lime wedges under the breast skin of the chicken and the rest inside the cavity with the remaining garlic half.
2. Place the chicken in the pan, breast-side down, brush with oil, and season. Add 2 tbsp/30ml of broth, cover with foil, and cook for 1 hour. Turn it over, baste, then roast for a further hour or until cooked; the juices should run clear when the thickest point of the thigh is pierced with a skewer or knife.
3. Remove the chicken from the pan. Strain the juices, skim off any excess fat, return to the pan, and stir in the flour. Cook gently for 1 minute, stirring, then add the remaining broth and simmer for 2 minutes, stirring. Serve the chicken with the juices spooned over the top.

Aromatic lime roast chicken

Ingredients

1 head garlic, cut in half crosswise
2 limes, cut into thin wedges
3 cardamom pods
1 tsp/5g cumin seeds
4 cloves

2lb12oz/1¼kg chicken, without giblets
2 tbsp/30ml olive oil
salt and black pepper
1 scant cup/7fl oz/200ml chicken broth
1 tbsp/15g all-purpose (plain) flour

Serves **4**

Method

1. Arrange the eggplant slices in layers in a colander, sprinkling salt over each layer. Set aside for 30 minutes. Rinse and pat dry with kitchen towels.
2. Preheat the oven to 400°F/200°C. Heat 2 tbsp/30ml of the oil in a frying pan, then fry the eggplant slices for 4–5 minutes, turning once, until softened and golden brown. Remove from the pan. Add 1 tbsp/15ml of oil to the pan, then fry the onion and garlic for 3–4 minutes, until softened and lightly browned.
3. Arrange a layer of tomatoes, a layer of eggplant, then a layer of onions in a shallow round ovenproof dish, 8in/20cm in diameter, seasoning each layer and sprinkling with thyme. Continue layering until all the vegetables are used, finishing with a layer of tomatoes. Drizzle with the remaining oil, then cook for 20 minutes. Sprinkle with Parmesan and cook for a further 5–10 minutes, until golden.

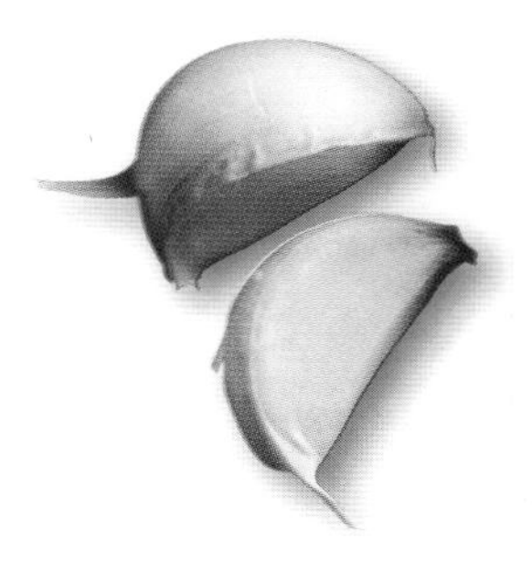

Eggplant and tomato bake

Ingredients

1 eggplant, thinly sliced

salt and black pepper

4 tbsp/60ml olive oil

1 onion, thinly sliced

2 cloves of garlic, finely chopped

6 plum tomatoes, thinly sliced

2 tbsp/30g chopped fresh thyme

3 tbsp/45g freshly grated Parmesan cheese

mediterranean

Serves **4**

Method

1. Preheat oven to 350°F/180°C.
2. Heat oil in frying pan and sauté garlic, tomatoes and onion until soft.
3. Add bell pepper, olives, thyme, tarragon, and wine. Cook, uncovered, for 5 minutes, over a moderate heat.
4. Place steaks in a greased, shallow, ovenproof dish. Pour sauce over steaks.
5. Cover and cook in the preheated moderate oven for 20 minutes, or until steaks are cooked through.

Ingredients

1 tbsp/15ml olive oil

3 tsp/15g crushed garlic

2 ripe tomatoes, chopped

1 small onion, minced

1 medium bell pepper, seeded, ribs discarded, finely chopped

Baked snapper niçoise

5 tbsp/65g black olives, pitted and finely sliced

¼ tsp/1.25g dried thyme leaves

½ tsp/2.5g dried tarragon leaves

1¾ cups/13fl oz/375ml dry white wine

4 red snapper or cod steaks

Serves **4**

Method

1. Slit each calamari tube along one side with a sharp knife. Cut it into large pieces and using a sharp knife score the underside in a diamond pattern but do not cut all the way through. Put 2 tbsp/25ml of olive oil, 3 cloves garlic, 2 red chili peppers, and the oregano in a bowl with the calamari pieces, cover and marinate in the refrigerator for 1–3 hours.

2. Put 5 tbsp/75ml of the oil, rosemary, 3 cloves garlic, and 1 chili pepper in a small saucepan and heat gently until the garlic just starts to turn golden. Strain the flavored oil and set aside.

3. Put the beans in another pot and heat through. Transfer half the beans to a food processor. In a slow steady stream, pour the flavored oil into the beans with the motor running. Fold the remaining whole beans into the puréed mixture. Set aside to keep warm. Discard the ingredients used to flavor the oil.

4. Heat the broiler until very hot, drain the excess oil from the calamari and broil under a high heat for a couple of minutes or until just cooked.

5. Fold the green onions (scallions) and parsley into the bean mixture, put a generous mound on each plate, and top with calamari pieces. Sprinkle with lemon juice and serve with arugula.

Ingredients

4 large calamari tubes, cleaned

⅓ cup/3½ fl oz/100ml extra virgin olive oil

6 cloves of garlic, crushed

3 small red chili peppers, finely sliced

2 tbsp/30g fresh oregano, chopped

1 sprig rosemary

Broiled calamari and bean mash salad

2½ cups/1 lb 5 oz/600g canned cannellini beans, rinsed and drained
4 green onions (scallions), finely sliced
2 tbsp/30g chopped flat-leaved parsley
2 tbsp lemon juice
arugula (rocket) leaves, to serve

Serves **4**

Method

1. Place the bread crumbs in a large bowl and combine with the ground beef, bacon, onion, parsley, egg, and seasoning and mix well. Shape the mixture into 20 balls and flatten slightly with the palm of your hand. Refrigerate for at least 10 minutes.
2. Heat the oil in a large frying pan and, over a medium to high heat, brown the meatballs on all sides for about 5 minutes (you may need to do this in two batches). Spoon off any excess oil from the frying pan and pour the pasta sauce over the meatballs in the pan. Reduce the heat to medium and simmer gently for 10 minutes, turning the meatballs occasionally, until cooked through.
3. Meanwhile, cook the pasta according to package instructions, then drain. Serve the meatballs with the pasta and garnish with extra parsley.

Meatballs with spicy tomato sauce

Ingredients

¼ cup/2 oz/50g fresh bread crumbs, made from 2 slices white loaf, crusts removed
2 cups/1¼ lb/500g lean ground beef
2oz/50g bacon, finely chopped
1 small onion, minced
3 tbsp chopped fresh parsley, plus extra, to garnish
1 medium egg, beaten
sea salt and freshly ground black pepper
2 tbsp/50ml sunflower oil
1¾ cups/14oz/390g spicy garlic pasta sauce
12oz/350g dried pasta, such as tagliatelle, fettucini, or penne

Serves **4**

Method

1. Preheat the oven to 220°C/425°F. Squeeze the juice from half the lemon and chop the other half into small pieces.

2. Toss the potatoes, lemon juice, chopped lemon, garlic, and oil together. Season, then arrange in a single layer in a shallow roasting pan and dot with the butter. Cook for 25–30 minutes, shaking the pan occasionally, until the potatoes are tender and golden brown. Stir in the olives just before serving.

Baby new potatoes with lemon and olives

Ingredients

1 lemon

1lb 11oz/750g baby new potatoes, halved if large

2 cloves of garlic, sliced

2 tbsp/30ml olive oil

salt and black pepper

2 tbsp/1oz/15g butter

2 tbsp/2oz/50g pitted green olives, quartered

mediterranean

Serves **4**

Method

1. Preheat the oven to 200°C/400°F. Cut four double-thickness, 15in/38cm squares of nonstick baking paper.

2. Heat the oil in a frying pan. Fry the onion and garlic for 2–3 minutes, until softened. Place a tablespoon of the mixture in the center of each square of paper. Top with a piece of cod, sprinkle with the parsley, then arrange the lemon slices on top.

3. Divide the tomatoes between the paper squares. Season, then spoon the wine over them. Lift opposite sides of the paper up and bring them over the filling, then fold over firmly at the top to make a sealed package. Place on a cookie sheet and bake for 20–25 minutes, until the fish is tender and cooked.

Baked cod packages

Ingredients

1 tbsp/15ml olive oil

1 small onion, thinly sliced

1 clove of garlic, thinly sliced

1lb 9oz/700g skinless cod fillet cut into 4 equal pieces

3 tbsp/45g chopped fresh parsley

1 lemon, thinly sliced

4 plum tomatoes, each cut lengthwise into 8 pieces

salt and black pepper

4 tbsp/60ml dry white wine

Serves **4**

Method

1. Preheat oven to 425°F/220°C. Place each fillet in center of a piece of aluminum foil about 12x16in/30x40cm. Drizzle 1 tbsp/15ml olive oil over each. Crumble equal amounts of cheese over each fillet and scatter olives on top. Sprinkle each fillet with a small amount of lemon juice and season with pepper.
2. Fold top of foil over bottom. Crimp edges tightly to seal. Arrange packages on a cookie sheet in a single layer. Bake for 10-12 minutes, or until foil is puffed and fish is cooked through.

Ingredients

4 red mullet fillets, 4–6½oz/125–185g each

4½ tbsp/65ml olive oil

½ cup/4oz/125g feta cheese

1 cup/8oz 250g black olives,pitted and coarsely chopped

2 tsp/10ml fresh lemon juice

cracked black pepper

Greek-style red mullet
with olives and feta cheese

Serves **4**

Method

1. Preheat the oven to 400°F/200°C. Finely grate the rind and squeeze the juice from 1 orange. Slice the top and bottom off the remaining orange, then cut away the peel and white parts, following the curve of the fruit. Cut between the membranes to release the segments, then chop the flesh.
2. Arrange the fennel and orange slices in a lightly greased shallow ovenproof dish and place the fish on top. Sprinkle with the orange juice and season.
3. Mix the chives with the orange rind, hazelnuts, bread crumbs, and oil. Season well and stir to mix evenly. Spoon the bread crumb mixture over the fish, smoothing to cover evenly. Bake for 35–40 minutes, or until the fish is cooked through and the topping is golden-brown.

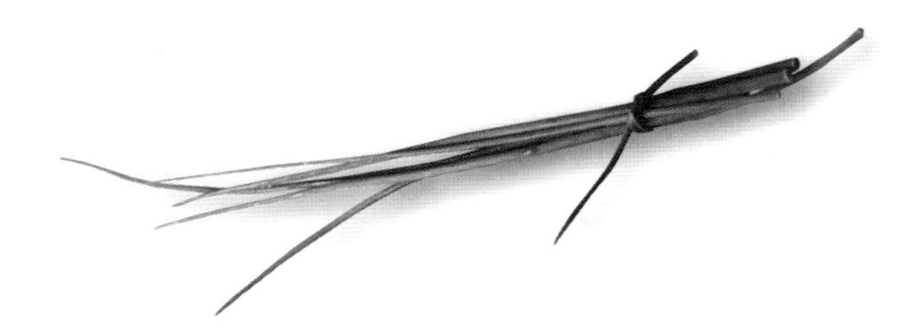

Baked monkfish
with hazelnut crumb topping

Ingredients

2 small oranges
1 small bulb fennel, thinly sliced
2 tbsp/30ml olive oil, plus extra for greasing
4 pieces monkfish fillet, about 5oz/150g each
salt and black pepper
2 tbsp/30g snipped fresh chives
2oz/50g whole blanched hazelnuts, chopped
2oz/50g fresh brown bread crumbs

mediterranean

Serves **4–6**

Method

Wash and pick over the chickpeas and soak overnight.

In a large saucepan, melt the butter and stir in the cinnamon, ginger, turmeric, paprika, pepper, and saffron threads. Cook slowly for two minutes to release the fragrance.

Add the cubed lamb, onion, parsley, and coriander and cook, stirring, until the lamb is brown and the onions are soft, about 15 minutes. Add the tomatoes and cook a further 5 minutes. Add the water and chickpeas and heat to boiling point. Simmer for 1 hour, partially covered.

Add the lentils and cook a further 45 minutes until the lentils are soft. Add lemon juice and salt and cook for a further 5 minutes. Serve with rice, lemon slices, and extra parsley if desired.

Ingredients

½ cup/4oz/125g chickpeas, washed, picked over and soaked overnight
2 tbsp/1oz/50g butter
1½ tsp/7.5g ground cinnamon
1 tsp/5g ground ginger
1 tsp/5g ground turmeric
1 tsp/5g ground paprika
½ tsp/2.5g ground black pepper
pinch of saffron threads
500g/1¼lb lamb fillets or shoulder, cut into cubes
1 large onion, minced
⅓ cup/3oz/85g chopped flatleaved parsley
⅓ cup/3oz/85g chopped coriander

Moroccan harira

1¾ cups/14oz/400g chopped canned tomatoes

5–6 cups water

½ cup/4oz/125g lentils, washed and picked over

2 tbsp lemon juice

salt to taste

lemon slices and extra chopped parsley,

to serve (optional)

Serves **4**

Method

1. To make the dressing, place the walnut oil and basil in a food processor, reserving a few basil leaves for garnish, and blend until smooth. Alternatively, use a hand mixer. Add the lime juice and blend again to combine.

2. Mix the pear with the beans and the prosciutto. Arrange on serving plates, season to taste, and scatter with the walnuts. Drizzle the dressing over the salad and garnish with the reserved basil leaves.

Bean salad
with basil and walnut dressing

Ingredients

1 red-skinned pear, such as Forelle or Blush, cored, quartered, and sliced into chunks crosswise

1¾ cups/14oz/400g canned flageolet beans, rinsed and drained

2½oz/70g prosciutto crudo (dry-cured ham), cut into strips

salt and black pepper

2 tbsp/30g walnut pieces

Dressing:

4 tbsp/60ml walnut oil

handful of fresh basil leaves

1 lime, juice squeezed

mediterranean

Serves **4**

Method

Heat butter and oil in a heavy-based pan.

Sauté onions and garlic, add rice, and sauté until well coated.

Add hot broth in small quantities, stir well, and gently simmer until the rice is creamy.

This takes about 20 minutes.

Stir in pork, mushrooms, cream, Parmesan, parsley, and bell pepper.

Taste and adjust accordingly. Leave to rest for 2–3 minutes.

Tip

Serve with lemon, toasted pine nuts, crispy prosciutto, and grated Parmesan.

Add 1 cup/8 fl oz/250ml water to 4 cups/1¾ pints/1 l chicken broth to reduce saltiness.

Ingredients

8oz/250g lean boneless pork,cubed

2 cups/8 oz/450g button mushrooms, sliced

½ cup/4fl oz/125ml light (single) cream

Risotto:

1 cup/8 fl oz/250ml white wine

5 cups/2 pints/1.25 l salt-reduced chicken broth

2 tbsp/1oz/50g butter

Pork and mushroom **risotto**

2 tbsp/30ml olive oil

1 onion, chopped

3 cloves of garlic, crushed

1½ cups/12oz/350g Arborio (short-grain, Italian) rice

½ cup/4oz/125g grated Parmesan cheese,

plus extra for serving

12 sprigs fresh parsley, chopped

¼ cup/2oz/50g chopped bell pepper

Serves **4**

Method

1. Place the chicken and peppers in a non-reactive bowl, add the lemon juice, garlic, olive oil, and coriander and mix well. Cover and leave to marinate for at least 1 hour. Meanwhile, combine all the ingredients for the sauce. Season and leave to chill. Soak four large wooden skewers in water for about 10 minutes.

2. Preheat the broiler to high. Thread the chicken and peppers onto the skewers and broil for 10–12 minutes, turning occasionally, until the chicken is slightly charred, cooked through, and tender. Keep warm.

3. Meanwhile, prepare the couscous according to package instructions, then fluff up with a fork. Melt the butter in a small saucepan and fry the green onions (scallions) for about 2 minutes. Add the green onions (scallions) with 3 tbsp/45g chopped coriander and plenty of seasoning to the couscous and mix well.
Serve the couscous on plates, with the kabobs on top, then drizzle with the yogurt sauce.

Chicken kebabs with couscous

Ingredients

4 chicken breast fillets,
skin removed, cut into 24 pieces
1 yellow and 1 red bell pepper
deseeded and cut into 8 pieces
1 lemon, rind grated, juice squeezed
2 cloves of garlic, crushed
2 tbsp/30ml extra virgin olive oil, sea salt and
freshly ground black pepper
1 tbsp/15g chopped fresh coriander

Couscous:
1 cup/250g/8oz couscous
2 tbsp/1 oz/25g butter
4 green onions (scallions), finely chopped
3 tbsp/45g chopped fresh coriander
sea salt and freshly ground, black pepper

Serves **4**

Method

1. Preheat the oven to 425°F/220°C/Gas Mark 7. For the topping, place the canned tomatoes in a saucepan. Simmer, uncovered, for 10–15 minutes, until reduced to a thick paste, stirring occasionally. Set aside while you make the base.
2. Mix the flour, salt, yeast, and sugar in a large bowl. Make a well in the center. Mix the oil with 1 scant cup/7fl oz/200ml of tepid water, then gradually pour into the well, drawing the flour from the edges to make a dough and adding more water if needed.
3. Turn out the dough onto a lightly floured surface and knead for 10 minutes or until smooth and elastic. Roll out to a 12in/30cm round and place on a greased baking sheet, pressing with your knuckles to make a slightly raised edge. Spread the cooked tomatoes over the pizza base and top with the salami or pepperoni, artichokes, plum tomatoes, mozzarella and olives. Cook for 20–25 minutes, until golden.

Ingredients

Base:

3 cups/12oz/350g all-purpose (strong plain) flour

1 tsp/5g salt

1 package active dry yeast

pinch of superfine (caster) sugar

2 tbsp/30ml olive oil

extra oil for greasing

Salami and artichoke pizza

Topping:

1¾ cups/14oz/400g canned chopped tomatoes with herbs

3 oz/100g peppered salami or pepperoni, cut into strips

1¼ cups/10oz/285g canned seasoned artichokes, drained

1 cup/9 oz/250g baby plum tomatoes, halved lengthways

3 oz/100g mozzarella, diced

2 tbsp/1oz/40g pitted black olives

Serves **4**

Method

1. Grease a shallow 8½in/22cm square roasting pan. Heat the butter and 1 tbsp/15ml of the oil in a large frying pan. Fry the zucchini (courgettes) for 3–4 minutes, until softened but not browned, stirring frequently. Remove from the heat.

2. Bring the broth to the boil in a large saucepan. Sprinkle with the polenta, stirring with a wooden spoon, and continue to stir for 5 minutes or until the polenta thickens and begins to come away from the sides of the pan. Remove from the heat and stir in the zucchini (courgettes). Season to taste.

3. Tip the polenta into the roasting pan, spreading evenly, then sprinkle with Parmesan and leave for 1 hour to cool and set.

4. Heat a ridged cast-iron grill pan over a high heat. Cut the polenta into slices, brush with the rest of the oil and cook for 2–4 minutes on each side, until golden. Alternatively, cook under a preheated broiler.

Zucchini polenta slices

Ingredients

1 tbsp/½ oz/15g butter, plus extra for greasing
3 tbsp/45ml olive oil
1 cup/8oz/250g courgettes, grated
3 cups/24fl oz/750ml chicken or vegetable broth
¾ cup/6oz/175g instant polenta
salt and black pepper
3 tbsp/1½oz/40g parmesan, finely grated

Serves **4**

Method

1. Preheat oven to 350°F/180°C.
2. Heat olive oil in a saucepan. Add onion and garlic, and cook until onion is transparent.
3. Add tarragon and tomato paste, and stir for 3–4 minutes. Add wine, tomatoes, anchovies and olives, and cook until tomatoes have broken up.
4. Cut 4 pieces of aluminum foil into 12in/30cm squares. Place foil shiny side down, and put fillet in the center.
5. Spoon sauce mixture on top of fillet. Bring opposite sides of foil together and pinch closed.
6. Bake in the oven for around 25 minutes.

Fish in putanesca sauce

Ingredients

Sauce:

20ml/4 tsp olive oil

1 large onion, finely diced

2 tsp/10g crushed garlic

2 tsp/10g dried tarragon leaves

1 tbsp/15ml tomato paste

½ cup/4fl oz/125ml white wine

1¾ cups/14 oz/400g whole, skinned tomatoes (fresh or canned)

4 anchovy fillets, finely chopped

½ cup/4 oz/125g pitted olives

4 white fish fillets (approximately 7 oz/200g each)

Serves **8–10**

Method

Cover the bulgur wheat with cold water and allow to stand for 30 minutes. Drain well, squeezing out any excess water. In a mixing bowl, combine the bulgur wheat, green onions (scallions), tomatoes, bell pepper, cucumber, parsley, and mint and mix well. Add the red pepper paste (see below) and mix thoroughly until the salad takes on a lovely red hue.

Whisk together the lemon juice, olive oil, pomegranate syrup, cumin, and salt and pepper. Pour the dressing over the vegetable mixture and toss thoroughly to make sure all the ingredients are coated. Add extra salt to taste if necessary then chill for 2 hours then serve cold or at room temperature.

To make the red pepper paste, place the bell peppers, chili peppers, water, salt, sugar, and olive oil in a food processor and process until smooth. Transfer the mixture to a saucepan and simmer gently until the mixture is thick and the liquid has reduced, about 1 hour, stirring frequently. Cool completely before use.

Ingredients

1½ cups fine bulgur wheat

1 bunch green onions (scallions), trimmed and finely sliced

2 large ripe tomatoes, seeded and diced

1 red bell pepper, seeded and diced

1 small cucumber, peeled, seeded and diced

1 packed cup (7oz/200g) minced parsley

¼ cup/1oz/2 tbsp sliced fresh mint

⅓ cup/3oz/100g red pepper paste (see below)

2 lemons, juice squeezed

¼ cup/2fl oz/50ml olive oil

1 tbsp pomegranate syrup

2 tsp/10g ground cumin

salt and pepper to taste

Turkish **tabbouleh** (Kisir)

Turkish red pepper paste:

4 red bell peppers, seeded and ribs discarded

4 red chili peppers

3 tbsp/40ml water

1 tsp/5g salt

1 tsp/5g sugar

4 tsp/20ml olive oil

Serves **4**

Method

1. Use a sharp knife to cut a deep slit in the side of each chicken breast, opening it out to form a pocket. Spoon the goat's cheese into the pockets and add a sprig of thyme to each. Fold the chicken over to enclose the cheese and secure the edges with wetted cocktail sticks.
2. Place the chicken breasts on a cookie sheet and brush with the honey. Season, then sprinkle with paprika. Broil for 7–8 minutes, or until golden-brown. Turn and cook the other side for a further 7–8 minutes, until tender and cooked through. Remove the cocktail sticks.
3. Meanwhile, toss the peppers and onion in the oil. Heat a ridged cast-iron grill pan and cook the vegetables for 3–4 minutes, until golden, turning once. Alternatively, or under a preheated broiler for the same amount of time. Sprinkle with the chopped thyme, spoon onto plates, and top with the chicken breasts. Sprinkle with a little paprika.

Honey-glazed chicken with goat's cheese

Ingredients

4 skinless, boneless chicken breasts
3½oz/100g soft goat's cheese
4 sprigs fresh thyme, plus
1 tsp/5g chopped fresh thyme
2 tbsp/30ml clear honey
salt and black pepper
½ tsp/2.5g paprika, plus extra to garnish
2 yellow bell peppers and 2 red bell peppers, deseeded and thickly sliced
1 red onion, thickly sliced
2 tbsp/30ml olive oil

mediterranean

Liver with red grapes

Serves **4**

Method

1. Mix together the flour, salt, and pepper on a plate. Dip the liver into the mixture to coat well. Heat the oil in a large, heavy-based frying pan. Add half the liver and cook for 2–3 minutes on each side, until cooked through. Remove from the pan and cook the remaining liver, then set aside.
2. Melt the butter in the pan until foaming, then stir in the sugar. Add the vinegar and stir vigorously, then add the broth and bring to the boil.
3. Lower the heat, add the grapes, and simmer for 4–5 minutes. Return the liver to the pan and reheat for 1–2 minutes, shaking the pan and spooning the sauce over the liver. Garnish with the parsley.

Ingredients

1–2 tbsp/15-30g all-purpose (plain) flour
salt and black pepper
1lb/450g thinly sliced lamb's or calf's liver
2 tbsp/30ml peanut oil
2 tbsp/1oz/25g butter
1 tbsp/15g brown sugar
2 tbsp/30ml raspberry or red wine vinegar
1 cup/9fl oz/250ml chicken broth
⅔ cup/5oz/150g seedless red or black grapes, halved if large
flat-leaved parsley to garnish

Serves **4**

Method

1. Preheat the oven to 375°F/190°C. Mix the breadcrumbs, parmesan cheese, green onions (scallions), lemon rind, butter, and seasoning together in a small bowl. Divide the mixture between the chicken breasts and using a fork, press the mixture down on top, to form an even coat.
2. Transfer the chicken breasts to a shallow roasting pan and bake for 20 minutes. Remove the chicken from the roasting pan and keep warm. Add the lemon juice and parsley to the buttery juices in the pan and mix well. Pour these juices over the chicken and serve immediately.

Oven-baked parmesan chicken

Ingredients

2 tbsp/1oz/25g fresh bread crumbs, made from 1 slice white bread, crusts removed
6 tbsp/3oz/75g parmesan cheese, finely grated
2 green onions (scallions), finely chopped
1 lemon, rind grated, juice squeezed
4 tbsp/2oz/50g butter, melted
sea salt and freshly ground black pepper
4 skinless chicken breast fillets
2 tbsp/30g chopped fresh parsley

mediterranean

Serves **4**

Method

Combine ground coriander, cumin, paprika, and chili paste and rub the mixture into the lamb. Heat half the oil in a large wok over medium-high heat, add half the lamb, and stir fry for 1–2 minutes, stirring continuously. Transfer to a plate and cover loosely with foil and set aside. Repeat with remaining lamb.

Reduce heat to medium, add remaining oil, and cook garlic for 2 minutes; add ginger and pumpkin and cook for 3 minutes, stirring continuously.

Return lamb to wok, add spinach, coriander, and lemon juice. Stir to combine and cook for 2 minutes to heat lamb through.

Serve immediately with couscous.

Moroccan spiced lamb

Ingredients

1¼ lb/500g lean lamb, cut into strips

2½ tsp/12.5g ground coriander

1½ tsp/7.5g ground cumin

1 tsp/5g ground sweet paprika

1 tsp/5ml chili paste

2½ tbsp/40ml vegetable oil

2 cloves of garlic cut into slices

1½ tsp/7.5g grated fresh ginger

1 cup/8 oz/250g pumpkin, cut into thin pieces/slices

1⅓ cups/3½ oz/100g spinach leaves

2 tbsp/30g freshly chopped coriander leaves

1tbsp/15ml fresh lemon juice

mediterranean

Serves **4**

Method

1. Heat 1¼ cups/10fl oz/300ml of the broth in a saucepan until boiling, then remove the pan from the heat and stir in the saffron threads.

2. Heat the oil and butter in a large heavy-based pan and gently fry the onion and garlic for 4–5 minutes, until softened but not browned. Add the rice and pumpkin or squash to the pan, and stir for 2 minutes or until the rice is coated with oil.

3. Stir in the wine and boil for a few seconds to cook off the alcohol, then pour in the saffron broth. Simmer, stirring constantly, for 5 minutes or until the broth has been absorbed. Add half the remaining broth and cook, stirring, for 10 minutes or until absorbed. Add the remaining broth and cook, stirring, for a further 10 minutes or until the rice is tender but still firm to the bite. Season.

4. Stir the lemon rind and juice and the Parmesan into the risotto, then garnish with rosemary.

Pumpkin, lemon, and parmesan risotto

Ingredients

4 cups/1¾ pints/1 l chicken or vegetable broth
Large pinch of saffron threads
2 tbsp/30ml olive oil
1 tbsp/½ oz/15g butter
1 onion, chopped
1 clove of garlic, finely chopped
1¾ cups/14oz/400g Italian risotto rice
2lb 4oz/1kg pumpkin or butternut squash, deseeded and cut into 2cm pieces
⅔ cup/5 fl oz/150ml dry white wine
salt and black pepper
1 lemon, rind grated squeezed
¼ cup/2oz/50g Parmesan, grated
½ tsp/2.5g finely chopped fresh rosemary to garnish

mediterranean

Serves **4**

Method

1. Preheat the oven to 375°F/190°C. Place the chicken in a roasting tray. Gently work the skin away from the flesh with your fingers and tuck about 6–7 basil leaves under the breast skin of the chicken. Place the remaining basil in a liquidizer with the olive oil, lemon juice and seasoning and whizz until smooth. Brush the chicken with half the basil oil and cook for 40 minutes.

2. Meanwhile, to prepare the onions, peel them and then slice off the root end to give a flat base. Make four cuts, in a criss-cross shape, across the top of each onion to come only halfway down, so that the onions open slightly. Combine the lemon rind with the garlic and sprinkle this over the onions.

3. Add the onions to the chicken in the pan and brush well with some of the basil oil. Brush the remaining oil over the chicken and cook for a further 40 minutes or until cooked through. Cover and allow the chicken to rest for 10 minutes before carving.

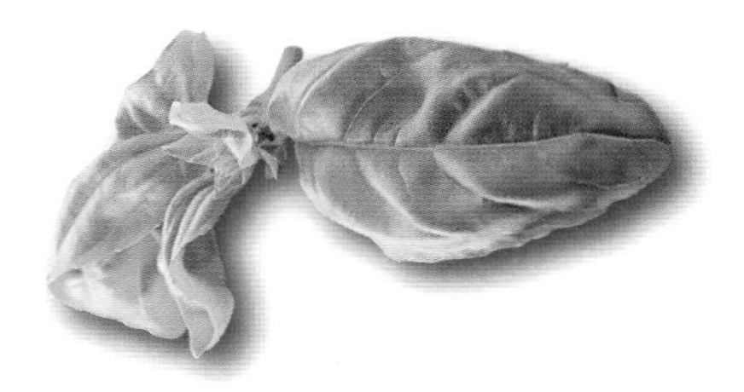

Roast chicken with basil and red onions

Ingredients

1 chicken, weighing about 3lb/2oz/1.4kg

1 tbsp/15g fresh basil

6 tbsp/90ml extra-virgin olive oil

Onions:

4 medium red onions

1 lemon, rind grated, juice squeezed

1 clove of garlic, crushed

sea salt and freshly ground black pepper

Serves **4–6**

Method

Heat the oil and brown pork in batches in a large hot frying pan, cooking for approximately 3–4 minutes. Remove and reserve.

Add onion to the frying pan and cook until soft. Add tomatoes, bell pepper, and sugar. Simmer, uncovered, to evaporate liquid for 4–5 minutes.

Stir in rice, broth, water, saffron, and bayleaf. Stir until boiling, then simmer uncovered for 10 minutes.

Add fish and mussels. Cover, simmer about 3 minutes.

Add pork and cook for a further 3–4 minutes. Gently stir rice and serve.

Pork & seafood **paella**

Ingredients

14oz/400g lean diced pork
1 tbsp/15ml olive oil
1 onion, finely chopped
2 tomatoes, chopped
1 green bell pepper, thinly sliced
1 tsp/5g sugar
2 cups/1 lb/450g long grain rice
2 cups/8 fl oz/250ml chicken broth
1½ cups/12fl oz/350ml water
pinch of saffron threads
1 bayleaf
7 oz/200g firm white fish (snapper, cod, grouper)
12–15 mussels
flatleaved parsley, to garnish

Serves **4**

Method

1. To make the marinade, place the garlic, yogurt, oil, cumin, coriander, paprika, cayenne pepper, and lemon juice in a large non-reactive bowl and mix well. Add the lamb, turning to coat. Cover and place in the fridge for 1 hour to marinate. If using wooden skewers, place them in water to soak for 10 minutes.
2. Stir the apricots and mint into the lamb and season. Thread the meat and apricots onto 8 metal or wooden skewers, placing a lemon wedge at both ends. Discard the marinade.
3. Preheat the broiler to high. Place the kabobs on a baking sheet under the broiler and cook for 8–10 minutes, turning occasionally, until the meat has browned. Spoon the juices over the kabobs and serve.

Spiced lamb and **apricot kebabs**

Ingredients

1lb/2oz/500g lean lamb, cut into1in/ 2.5cm pieces

½ cup/4oz/125g ready-to-eat dried apricots

1 tbsp/15g finely chopped fresh mint

salt and black pepper

1 lemon, cut into 8 wedges

Marinade:

1 clove of garlic, crushed

2 tbsp/30ml low-fat plain yogurt

1 tbsp/15ml olive oil, 1 tsp/5g ground cumin

1 tsp/5g ground coriander

1 tsp/5g paprika

pinch of cayenne pepper

1 lemon, juice squeezed

Serves **4**

Method

Preheat the oven to 400°F/200°C. Trim the asparagus and remove any woody ends of the stems. Put the asparagus in a single layer in a baking pan, sprinkle it with the olive oil, and shake to evenly cover.

Add salt and pepper, cover the pan, and bake 20–25 minutes in the oven, until the asparagus is done.

Meanwhile, combine the mayonnaise, pesto, pistachios, and the garlic. Add salt and pepper and serve the pistachio mayonnaise with the baked asparagus.

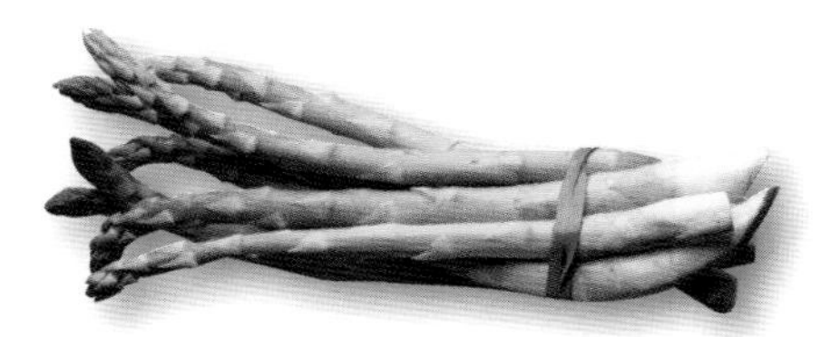

Asparagus with hollandaise sauce

Ingredients

1lb 10oz/750g thick green asparagus

3 tbsp/45ml olive oil

salt and black pepper

Sauce:

5 tbsp/75ml mayonnaise

1 tbsp/15ml green pesto

⅓ cup/2¾ oz/75 g pistachios, finely chopped

1 clove of garlic, minced

Serves **4**

Method

Add the saffron threads to the hot broth and allow to rest.

Heat the olive oil in a large saucepan and add the paprika, chili, turmeric, and garlic. Cook for 1 minute to release the aroma of the spices. Add the onions and chicken and cook until onions are very soft and the chicken juices run clear.

Add the rice and stir to coat, followed by the wine. Stir frequently, while the wine is being absorbed. When all the liquid has disappeared, add the tomato paste, parsley, and orange rind and juice. Continue cooking and stirring, adding the broth half a cup/4 fl oz/125ml at a time, stirring well after each addition. Continue in this manner until all the broth has been absorbed and the rice is firm but tender. Remove the saucepan from the heat, add the finely sliced green onions (scallions), plenty of fresh herbs, and black pepper, and serve immediately.

Spanish **rice**

Ingredients

2 tbsp/ olive oil

2 tbsp mild paprika

¼ tsp chili pepper flakes or ½ tsp fresh chili pepper

1 tsp/5g turmeric

good pinch of saffron threads

2 onions, sliced thinly

4 cloves of garlic, minced

2 skinless boneless chicken breasts

1 orange, rind grated, juice squeezed

1¾ cups/14oz/400g arborio rice

6fl oz/180ml white wine

3⅔ cups/1½ pints/900ml rich vegetable, chicken or beef broth, simmering

2 tbsp/30ml tomato paste

½ cup/2 oz/50g chopped parsley

4 green onions (scallions), minced

extra fresh herbs

freshly ground black pepper

mediterranean

Serves **4**

Method

1. Shell the shrimp, then slit open the back of each one and scrape out the black vein. Rinse well and pat dry with kitchen towels.
2. Heat the oil in a large frying pan and fry the garlic and chili peppers gently for 1 minute to release their flavor. Add the shrimp and stir-fry over a medium to high heat for 3 minutes or until the shrimp have turned pink and are cooked through.
3. Stir in the fresh and dried tomatoes and simmer for 1 minute, then remove from the heat and add the wine vinegar, olives and basil. Season.

Tiger shrimp
with provençal tomato salsa

Ingredients

14oz/400g raw tiger prawns
2 tbsp/30ml olive oil
1 clove of garlic, finely chopped
½ tsp dried crushed chilies
3 plum tomatoes, finely chopped
4 sun-dried tomatoes in oil, drained and finely chopped
2 tsp/10ml red wine vinegar
6 pitted black olives, quartered
2 tbsp/30g chopped fresh basil
salt and black pepper

mediterranean

Serves **4**

Method

1. Heat the oil in a large heavy-based saucepan, then add the garlic, chili pepper flakes, if using, onions, eggplant, zucchini, and fennel. Stir well, and cook, covered, for 10 minutes, stirring often, or until the vegetables have softened.

2. Add the yellow pepper, tomatoes, lemon juice, sugar, oregano, and seasoning to the onion mixture. Simmer, uncovered, for 10 minutes or until all the vegetables are tender, stirring occasionally.

Ratatouille in fresh tomato sauce

Ingredients

3 tbsp/45ml olive oil, 2 cloves of garlic, sliced

½ tsp/2.5g chili flakes (optional)

2 red onions, sliced

1 large eggplant (aubergine), cut into ¼in/1cm cubes, 2 zucchini (courgettes), cut into ½ in/1cm cubes

1 fennel bulb cut into ½ in/1cm cubes

1 yellow bell pepper deseeded and cut into ½in/1cm cubes

6 plum tomatoes, chopped

1 lemon, juice squeezed

1 tbsp soft light or dark, brown sugar

1 tsp/5g dried oregano, black pepper

Serves **6–8**

Method

Preheat oven to 200°C. Sift flour into a bowl and, using your finger tips, work the butter into the flour (until the mixture resembles breadcrumbs). Add the egg and water and combine to a biscuit, crumb-like dough. Rollout pastry and use to line a 22 cm false-bottom flan-dish. Prick the base of the pastry, cover and chill for 20 minutes.

For the filling: Beat together the butter and sugar until light and creamy. Add the egg and continue beating. Stir in the almonds, lemon rind and plain flour. Spread evenly over the base of the tart and arrange the dates.

Place on a baking tray. Bake for 12 minutes then reduce heat to 180°C and continue baking for a further 20 minutes, or until the base has set and the tart is golden brown.

Brush the tart lightly with rose water whilst still warm. Serve hot or cold

Ingredients

250g plain flour

75g butter

1 egg

1tbsp chilled water

Filling:

250g butter

2 eggs, beaten

180g ground almonds

rind of 1 lemon, finely grated

2 tbsp plain flour

12 fresh dates, stoned and halved

rose water to glaze

Date and rosewater **tart**

Method

Preheat the oven to 350°F/180°C and butter a 8in/20cm nonstick springform pan.

Place the butter and chocolate, broken into pieces, into a heatproof bowl and set over a saucepan of simmering water or melt in a microwave oven on defrost setting. Stir gently until the chocolate is thoroughly melted and the mixture is smooth. Beat in the coffee powder and cocoa then set aside.

In a separate bowl, beat the eggs and sugar together until thick and pale, about 5 minutes, then fold in the ground walnuts and walnut pieces.

Gently fold the chocolate mixture into the egg mixture until thoroughly combined, then pour the batter into the prepared cake pan.

Bake for 40 minutes or until the top of the cake is dry. Turn off the oven and leave the cake undisturbed to cool.

When the cake is cool, remove from the cold oven and gently remove from the pan. Dust with a combination of the cocoa and powdered sugar and serve in thin slices.

Torta di cioccolata

Italian-style chocolate cake

Ingredients

½ cup/3½ oz/100g butter

12oz/350g semi-sweet baking chocolate

1 tbsp/5g instant coffee powder

3 tbsp/45g unsweetened cocoa powder

5 large eggs

1 cup/8oz/250g caster sugar

5 tbsp ground walnuts

½ cup/3½ oz/100g walnut pieces

Topping:

1 tbsp/15 g unsweetened cocoa powder

1 tbsp/15 g powdered (icing) sugar

mediterranean

Method:

Preheat the oven to 375°F/190°C.

Using 3 tbsp/¾oz/20g of butter from the total quantity, grease a 10in/24cm cake pan generously, then sprinkle with the ground walnuts. Set aside.

Peel, core, and quarter the apples, then cut them into slices. Toss the apples with the lemon rind and juice and set aside.

Whisk the eggs, vanilla, and sugar together until pale and creamy, then add the melted butter, flour, baking powder, and milk. Mix thoroughly.

Pour one third of the batter into the prepared cake pan, then top with one third of apple, raisins, and pine nuts. Repeat with remaining ingredients. Finish with layer of apples. Combine the sugar and cinnamon then sprinkle the mixture over the top. Bake for 55 minutes, then allow to cool in the pan for 20 minutes. Unmold and sprinkle with powdered sugar before serving.

Ingredients:

½ cup/4oz/120g butter, melted

2 tbsp/50g toasted walnuts, ground

5 cups 2¼lb/1kg tart green apples (such as granny smith)

1 lemon, rind grated, juice squeezed

3 large eggs

2 tsp/10ml vanilla extract

1 cup/8oz/250g sugar

1⅓ cups/5½ oz/150g flour

2 tsp/10g baking powder

⅓ cup/3½ fl oz/100ml milk

½ cup/4oz/120g raisins

⅓ cup/3½oz/100g pine nuts, toasted

3 tbsp/45g sugar

1 tsp/5g cinnamon

1 tbsp icing sugar

Torta siciliana di mele
Sicilian apple cake

Serves **6**

Method

1. Preheat the oven to 350°F/180°C. Melt the butter in a saucepan, then stir in the graham crackers and almonds. Press into the base of a deep, lightly greased 8in/20 cm loose-bottomed cake pan. Bake for 10 minutes.
2. Meanwhile, finely grate the rind and squeeze the juice from 2 of the lemons. Blend with the ricotta, yogurt, eggs, cornstarch, and sugar in a food processor until smooth, or beat with a hand whisk. Pour the mixture over the cookie base and bake for 45–50 minutes, until lightly set and golden. Cool in the pan for at least an hour, then run a knife around the edge to loosen and turn out onto a serving platter.
3. Thinly slice the remaining lemon. Place in a saucepan, cover with boiling water and simmer for 5 minutes, then drain. Heat the honey over a low heat – but do not let it boil. Dip the lemon slices in the honey and arrange over the cheesecake.

Lemon ricotta cheesecake

Ingredients

¼ cup/2oz/50g butter

3½oz/100g graham crackers (digestive biscuits) crushed

1½oz/40g ground almonds

3 lemons

1 cup/8oz/250g ricotta

⅔ cup/5oz/150g Greek yogurt

3 eggs

1 tbsp/15g cornstarch

3oz/75g caster sugar

1 tbsp/15ml clear honey

mediterranean

Index